Get Around

with Cargo

Get Around
with Cargo

by Lee Sullivan Hill

Carolrhoda Books, Inc./Minneapolis

To my husband, Gary, with love.
—L.S.H.

For more information about the photographs in this book, see the Photo Index on pages 30–32.

The photographs in this book are reproduced through the courtesy of: © Howard Ande, cover, pp. 5, 16, 17, 19, 20, 21; © Eugene G. Schulz, pp. 1, 6, 8, 9, 11, 12, 14, 29; © Bob Firth/Firth Photobank, pp. 2, 7, 15, 18; © Buddy Mays/Travel Stock, pp. 10, 13, 27; © David Clobes, pp. 22, 23; © Kimberly Burnham/Unicorn Stock Photos, p. 24; © Eric R. Berndt/Unicorn Stock Photos, p. 25; ©John S. Reid, p. 26; © NASA, p. 28.

Carolrhoda Books, Inc.
A Division of the Lerner Publishing Group
241 First Avenue North, Minneapolis, MN 55401 U.S.A.

Website address: www.lernerbooks.com

Library of Congress Cataloging-in-Publication Data

Hill, Lee Sullivan, 1958–
    Get around with cargo / by Lee Sullivan Hill.
       p.   cm. — (A get around book)
    Includes index.
    Summary: Briefly describes some of the methods used to move goods from one place to another, including pack animals, barges and other boats, trains, and trucks.
    ISBN 1-57505-311-X
    1. Freight and freightage—Juvenile literature. 2. Cargo handling—Juvenile literature. [1. Freight and freightage. 2. Cargo handling. 3. Transportation.] I. Title. II. Series: Hill, Lee Sullivan, 1958– Get around book.
HE199.A2H55 1999   99-17150
388'.044-dc21

Manufactured in the United States of America
1 2 3 4 5 6 – SP – 04 03 02 01 00 99

A train rumbles down the tracks. It carries cargo across the countryside.

Loads of goods that people need are called cargo. Cargo can be heaps of sugarcane, sent from farms to factories.

Cargo can be cars stacked high. They travel from factories to buyers. Transportation moves things from where they are made to where they are used.

Sometimes people carry goods themselves. People
haul rice or vegetables from their farms to sell in town.

Bikes help people move more cargo. The bike wheels roll along, and the cargo takes a ride.

Animals help haul loads, too. Llamas carry packs
strapped to their backs.

Cattle pull carts loaded with bags of grain—and a family along for the ride.

Some loads are far too big for animals. Boats float heavy loads on water. They carry tons of cargo.

Huge ships travel over ocean waters. They carry goods such as steel, logs, cars, and oil.

Small boats haul loads around a harbor. People can
sell their goods from a boat.

Big barges piled with cargo are pushed along by tugboats. They slip downriver to harbors near the sea.

When cargo must cross land, trains can do the job.
Engines in front pull a long line of railroad cars.

Each kind of railroad car carries a different kind of cargo. Hopper cars haul dry goods such as grain.

Flat cars can be stacked with goods that have odd shapes. Farm equipment is strapped on for the trip.

Tanker cars carry liquids. Some hold corn syrup,
which is used to make juice and cookies.

Trains stay on tracks, but trucks get around all over land. Farmers drive trucks right onto their fields when it's time to harvest crops.

Mail trucks carry letters and packages to people everywhere.

Tanker trucks pull up to cow barns. They haul fresh milk to a dairy.

Pick-up trucks handle all kinds of loads. The bed of the truck holds boxes and hay. A horse trailer hooks on the back.

Huge boxes called containers travel by ship, train, and truck. Cargo stays in the container, while a crane swings it from ship to train.

Trains haul containers across the country. Later, each container will hook up to a truck for the final delivery.

Sometimes cargo must travel more quickly. Jets carry important letters and live lobsters. The cargo gets there overnight.

Small planes carry goods to people who live far from roads and cities.

Cargo travels by land, sea, and air—even into space!
Shuttles bring supplies to astronauts up in space.

Out in space or down a dirt road, transportation moves the goods people need.

Photo Index

Cover This train is making its way along the Golden State Railway near Newkirk, New Mexico. It hauls cargo in huge boxes called containers. Read more about containers on pages 24 and 25.

Page 6 The panel sides of this truck in Puerto Rico keep freshly harvested stalks of sugarcane from spilling out along curvy mountain roads. Sugarcane is transported from mountain plantations to sugar factories near the coast.

Page 1 This camel is hitched to a loaded cart in Jaipur, India. The cart and its wheels allow the camel to pull a heavier load than it could carry on its back.

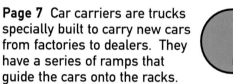

Page 7 Car carriers are trucks specially built to carry new cars from factories to dealers. They have a series of ramps that guide the cars onto the racks. This car carrier is traveling through eastern North Dakota.

Page 2 Ore boats carry iron ore from mines to steel mills. This one is headed into the harbor at Duluth, Minnesota. Ore boats often travel over canals in the Great Lakes region of the United States.

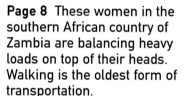

Page 8 These women in the southern African country of Zambia are balancing heavy loads on top of their heads. Walking is the oldest form of transportation.

Page 5 A train loaded with coal rolls through La Fox, Illinois. The railcars, called hopper cars, are shaped like funnels. Hinged doors in the bottoms of the cars will open when it's time to unload the coal.

Page 9 Bikes help these farmers get their harvest to market in Shanghai, China. How many kinds of cargo-moving vehicles with wheels can you find in this book?

Page 10 Camping gear is strapped to the backs of these llamas traveling with a group of trekkers on the Continental Divide Trail in Colorado. Llamas, native to South America, have served as pack animals for hundreds of years.

Page 11 This team of oxen in rural Zambia helps a man and four boys bring heavy sacks home to their village. Farmers use strong, sturdy oxen to pull carts, wagons, and plows.

Page 12 This boat took on its cargo at Cheung Chau Island, Hong Kong. The hydraulic crane at the front of the boat helps load bundles and packages.

Page 13 This ship is sailing from Japan to New York through the Panama Canal—the shortcut that connects the Atlantic and Pacific Oceans. Before the canal was built, ships had to sail all the way around South America.

Page 14 Many families live in Hong Kong Harbor on boats called sampans. This vendor travels from one sampan to the next, selling food to families.

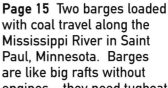

Page 15 Two barges loaded with coal travel along the Mississippi River in Saint Paul, Minnesota. Barges are like big rafts without engines—they need tugboats to move them.

Page 16 Three diesel engines pull this train over mountains in New York State. They are headed across the Hudson River on their way to New York City.

Page 17 Grain flows into a hopper car at the Farmer's Co-op in Moweaqua, Illinois. The car has a cover to keep out birds and debris. Hopper cars used for coal, like the ones on page 5, have open tops.

Page 18 Engineers, dispatchers, and mechanics are some of the people who keep trains working. The National Academy of Railroad Sciences in Overland Park, Kansas, trains students to work in the railroad industry.

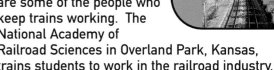

Page 19 This line of tanker cars is headed south out of Chicago, Illinois. More rail cargo passes through Chicago than any other city in the United States.

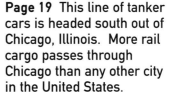

Page 20 At harvesttime in Ancona, Illinois, a John Deere 9600 combine is filling a dump truck with soybeans. Dump trucks tilt up in the air to unload, or dump, their cargo.

Page 21 The United States Postal Service transports mail in trucks like this one, which is traveling near Nara Visa, New Mexico. They also ship mail in boxcars hooked to passenger trains and in cargo jets.

Page 22 This stainless steel tanker truck pumps milk from holding tanks at a dairy farm in Mankato, Minnesota. A refrigerator unit keeps the milk cold during its trip to a dairy, where it will be processed.

Page 23 In the past, horses were often used to pull cargo. People now use horses more often for pleasure riding. In this picture, the horse is the cargo, on its way to its new owner in Cannon Falls, Minnesota.

Page 24 Containers carry almost any kind of cargo you can imagine. The ship *Americana* unloads containers in Miami, Florida.

Page 25 When cargo moves from sea to rail to road in containers, it is called intermodal transportation. Intermodal transportation saves time and money because smaller packages are handled less often.

Page 26 This cargo plane in Ontario, California, is a Boeing 747 owned by United Parcel Service. Have you ever seen brown UPS trucks where you live? Trucks make local deliveries, and jets fly the cargo between cities.

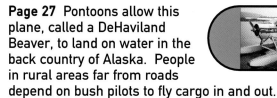

Page 27 Pontoons allow this plane, called a DeHaviland Beaver, to land on water in the back country of Alaska. People in rural areas far from roads depend on bush pilots to fly cargo in and out.

Page 28 Russian cosmonaut Nikolai M. Budarian took this photo on July 4, 1995, just after the space shuttle *Atlantis* finished docking with *Mir*, the Russian space station. *Atlantis* delivered supplies to astronauts on *Mir*.

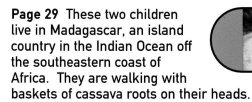

Page 29 These two children live in Madagascar, an island country in the Indian Ocean off the southeastern coast of Africa. They are walking with baskets of cassava roots on their heads.